Ten
of Happiness

ex libris

Candlestick Press

Published by:
Candlestick Press,
Diversity House, 72 Nottingham Road, Arnold, Nottingham NG5 6LF
www.candlestickpress.co.uk

Design and typesetting by Craig Twigg

Printed by Ratcliff & Roper Print Group, Nottinghamshire, UK

Selection and Introduction © Deborah Alma, 2019
https://emergencypoet.com

Cover illustration © Victoria McGrane, 2019
www.thescenicroutestyle.com

Candlestick Press monogram © Barbara Shaw, 2008

© Candlestick Press, 2019
Reprinted 2020, 2021, 2022

ISBN 978 1 907598 73 9

Acknowledgements:

The poems in this pamphlet are reprinted from the following books, all by
permission of the publishers listed unless stated otherwise. Every effort has been
made to trace the copyright holders of the poems published in this book. The
editor and publisher apologise if any material has been included without
permission or without the appropriate acknowledgement, and would be glad to be
told of anyone who has not been consulted.

Thanks are due to all the copyright holders cited below for their kind permission:

Deborah Alma, first published in this pamphlet. Meg Cox, *Looking Over My
Shoulder at Sodom* (Grey Hen Press, 2014). Jonathan Davidson, *Early Train*
(Smith|Doorstop, 2011). Tony Hoagland, *Unincorporated Persons in the Late
Honda Dynasty.* Copyright © 2010 by Tony Hoagland. Reprinted with the
permission of The Permissions Company, Inc., on behalf of Graywolf Press,
Minneapolis, Minnesota, www.graywolfpress.org. Jane Kenyon, *Collected
Poems.* Copyright © 2005 by The Estate of Jane Kenyon. Reprinted with the
permission of The Permissions Company LLC on behalf of Graywolf Press,
www.graywolfpress.org. Bryony Littlefair, *Giraffe* (Seren Books, 2018). Naomi
Shihab Nye, *Selected Poems* (Far Corner Books, 1995). RS Thomas, *Collected
Poems: 1945-1995* (Orion Books, 2012). James Wright, *Above the River:
Complete Poems* (FSG; Bloodaxe Books, 1992).

All permissions cleared courtesy of Swift Permissions
(swiftpermissions@gmail.com).

Where poets are no longer living, their dates are given.

Contents

Introduction

"Now and then it's good to pause in our pursuit of happiness and just be happy." So said the French poet Guillaume Apollinaire whose life was short but vividly rich and adventurous.

In my alter ego of Emergency Poet, I am often asked to prescribe poetry to counteract the stresses of modern day living; the mortgage, the kids, their school, the unreasonable boss, the state of politics and on and on.

The poems that I prescribe remind people to sit still, to look around them, to appreciate the small sacrament of the everyday; the cup of tea in a garden, the book at bedtime, to take pleasure in fresh bed-linen and the sound of birdsong, even in the city.

The poems I have chosen for this happy little book remind us of Apollinaire's wisdom, remind us to stop and notice that there might be happiness already if we could only see it. They range across some of the many things we might understand as happiness; from Meg Cox's moments of joy and laughter in 'The Best Medicine' to Tony Hoagland's 'Field Guide' where the poet helps us to find it just by noticing something beautiful.

My own poem 'Silence' is not really about being quiet but about contentment, and then there is Jane Kenyon's version in 'Happiness' which shows us something hopeful – deeper, more difficult happiness and how it can be hard to spot in our everyday lives. There is happiness in hope and in nature, happiness in "a boy's cheerfulness" and then there's the giraffe...

Deborah Alma

So Much Happiness
(for Michael)

It is difficult to know what to do with so much happiness.
With sadness there is something to rub against,
a wound to tend with lotion and cloth.
When the world falls in around you, you have pieces to pick up,
something to hold in your hands, like ticket stubs or change.

But happiness floats.
It doesn't need you to hold it down.
It doesn't need anything.
Happiness lands on the roof of the next house, singing,
and disappears when it wants to.
You are happy either way.
Even the fact that you once lived in a peaceful tree house
and now live over a quarry of noise and dust
cannot make you unhappy.
Everything has a life of its own,
it too could wake up filled with possibilities
of coffee cake and ripe peaches,
and love even the floor which needs to be swept,
the soiled linens and scratched records...

Since there is no place large enough
to contain so much happiness,
you shrug, you raise your hands, and it flows out of you
into everything you touch. You are not responsible.
You take no credit, as the night sky takes no credit
for the moon, but continues to hold it, and share it,
and in that way, be known.

Naomi Shihab Nye

A Short Piece of Choral Music

It's an evening in late March and in the kitchen
I'm listening to a short piece of choral music,
when my son comes in to fetch himself a bowl
of breakfast cereal which, he tells me, helps
with his revision. And another thing, he goes on,
I shouldn't worry about him because he's going
to be fine: exams, work, life, everything, is going
to be fine. That's a relief, I say to myself, thanks,
now I can listen to this music, which turns out
to be just some fancy noise, nothing
compared with a boy's cheerfulness.

Jonathan Davidson

Field Guide

Once, in the cool blue middle of a lake,
up to my neck in that most precious element of all,

I found a pale-gray, curled-upwards pigeon feather
floating on the tension of the water

at the very instant when a dragonfly,
like a blue-green iridescent bobby pin,

hovered over it, then lit, and rested.
That's all.

I mention this in the same way
that I fold the corner of a page

in certain library books,
so that the next reader will know

where to look for the good parts.

Tony Hoagland (1953 – 2018)

A Blessing

Just off the highway to Rochester, Minnesota,
Twilight bounds softly forth on the grass.
And the eyes of those two Indian ponies
Darken with kindness.
They have come gladly out of the willows
To welcome my friend and me.
We step over the barbed wire into the pasture
Where they have been grazing all day, alone.
They ripple tensely, they can hardly contain their happiness
That we have come.
They bow shyly as wet swans. They love each other.
There is no loneliness like theirs.
At home once more,
They begin munching the young tufts of spring in the darkness.
I would like to hold the slenderer one in my arms,
For she has walked over to me
And nuzzled my left hand.
She is black and white,
Her mane falls wild on her forehead,
And the light breeze moves me to caress her long ear
That is delicate as the skin over a girl's wrist.
Suddenly I realize
That if I stepped out of my body I would break
Into blossom.

James Wright (1927 – 1980)

The Best Medicine

It must be genetic
that just lying on our backs
made me and my brother laugh.
When we had adjoining bedrooms
our mother would shout up the stairs
'stop reading now and go to sleep'.
Later she would shout again
'stop laughing now'.

Adult, I went to yoga classes
and at the end we had to lie
on our backs on our mats and relax
doing yogic breathing, but before long
I was asked to leave before that part –
disruptive to meditation.

Come to think of it
lying on my back laughing
has caused me quite a bit of trouble
in the past.

Meg Cox

Happiness

There's just no accounting for happiness,
or the way it turns up like a prodigal
who comes back to the dust at your feet
having squandered a fortune far away.

And how can you not forgive?
You make a feast in honor of what
was lost, and take from its place the finest
garment, which you saved for an occasion
you could not imagine, and you weep night and day
to know that you were not abandoned,
that happiness saved its most extreme form
for you alone.

No, happiness is the uncle you never
knew about, who flies a single-engine plane
onto the grassy landing strip, hitchhikes
into town, and inquires at every door
until he finds you asleep mid afternoon
as you so often are during the unmerciful
hours of your despair.

It comes to the monk in his cell.
It comes to the woman sweeping the street
with a birch broom, to the child
whose mother has passed out from drink.
It comes to the lover, to the dog chewing
a sock, to the pusher, to the basketmaker,
and to the clerk stacking cans of carrots
in the night.
　　　　　It even comes to the boulder
in the perpetual shade of pine barrens,
to rain falling on the open sea,
to the wineglass, weary of holding wine.

Jane Kenyon (1947 – 1995)

Arrival

Not conscious
that you have been seeking
suddenly
you come upon it

the village in the Welsh hills
dust free
with no road out
but the one you came in by.

A bird chimes
from a green tree
the hour that is no hour
you know. The river dawdles
to hold a mirror for you
where you may see yourself
as you are, a traveller
with the moon's halo
above him, whom has arrived
after long journeying where he
began, catching this
one truth by surprise
that there is everything to look forward to.

RS Thomas (1913 – 2000)

How happy is the little Stone

How happy is the little Stone
That rambles in the Road alone,
And doesn't care about Careers,
And Exigencies never fears –
Whose Coat of elemental Brown
A passing Universe put on,
And independent as the sun,
Associates or glows alone,
Fulfilling absolute Decree
In casual simplicity –

Emily Dickinson (1830 – 1886)

Giraffe

When you feel better from this – and you will – it will be quiet and unremarkable, like walking into the next room. It might sting a little, like warmth leaking into cold-numbed hands. When you feel better, it will be the slow clearing of static from the radio. It will be a film set when the director yells *cut!* When you feel better, you will take: a plastic spoon for your coffee foam, free chocolates from the gleaming oak reception desk, the bus on sunny days, your own sweet time. When you feel better, it will be like walking barefoot on cool, smooth planks of wood, still damp from last night's rain. It will be the holy silence when the tap stops dripping. The moment a map finally starts to make sense. When you feel better, you will still suffer, but your sadness will be graspable, roadworthy, have handlebars. When you feel better, you will not always be happy, but when happiness does come, it will be long-legged, sun-dappled: a giraffe.

Bryony Littlefair

Silence

We stopped the car on the mountain pass,
too high for birds and out of the wind

crossed the road, still looked both ways,
although we hadn't seen another car for ten miles

and still your old habit of taking my hand to cross
and I slipped off my glove to feel the warmth.

My shoes tap tapped across the tarmac
and you kicked a loose stone, which dull-clattered

to a halt and there it was, something beautiful,
something I had been chasing all my life

had driven very far to find,
without even knowing it.

Deborah Alma